Theory Paper   Grade 1   2018   A
Model Answers

1   (10)

(a)

(b)

2   (10)

3   (10)

(a) C   E   D   A   G   F   B♭   C   F

(b) crotchet / quarter note

4   (10)

Key   C major

Key   G major

Key   D major

5 (10)

(a)

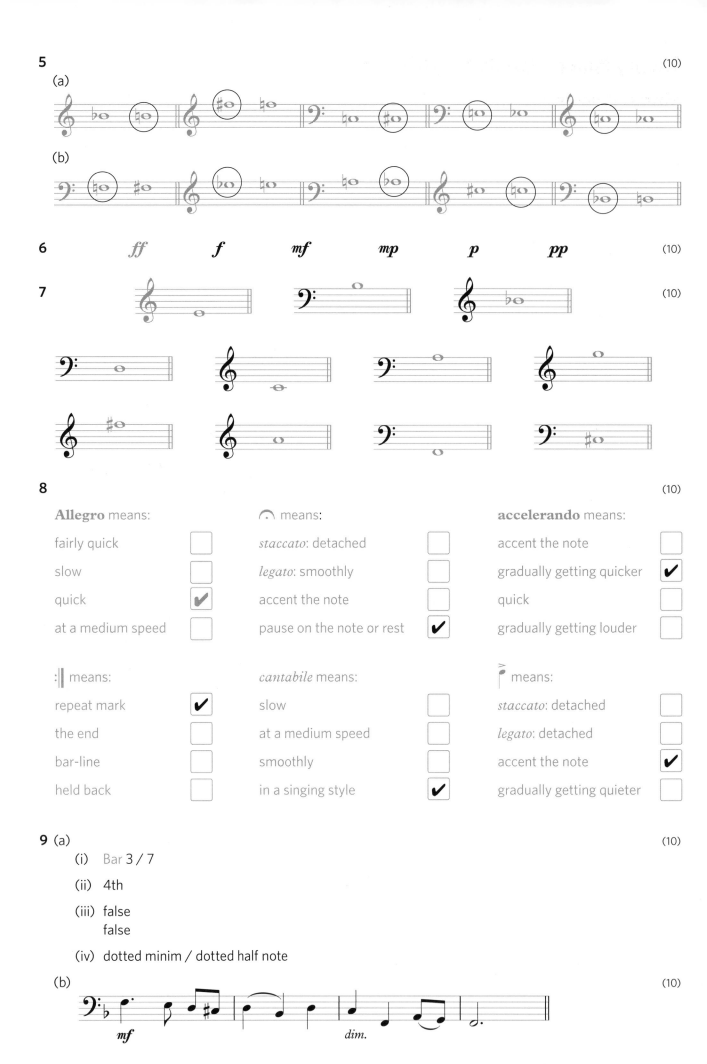

(b)

6 ***ff*** ***f*** ***mf*** ***mp*** ***p*** ***pp*** (10)

7 (10)

8 (10)

Allegro means:

fairly quick	☐
slow	☐
quick	✔
at a medium speed	☐

⌢ means:

staccato: detached	☐
legato: smoothly	☐
accent the note	☐
pause on the note or rest	✔

accelerando means:

accent the note	☐
gradually getting quicker	✔
quick	☐
gradually getting louder	☐

:‖ means:

repeat mark	✔
the end	☐
bar-line	☐
held back	☐

cantabile means:

slow	☐
at a medium speed	☐
smoothly	☐
in a singing style	✔

⸙ means:

staccato: detached	☐
legato: detached	☐
accent the note	✔
gradually getting quieter	☐

9 (a) (10)

(i) Bar 3 / 7

(ii) 4th

(iii) false
false

(iv) dotted minim / dotted half note

(b) (10)

mf *dim.*

4

Theory Paper   Grade 1   2018   B
Model Answers

1 (10)

2 (10)

3 (10)

(a)

(b)

4   D major   G major   F major   (10)

C major   F major   G major

5 (10)

6 (10)

7 (10)

(a) 3rd   1st /   2nd   4th   3rd   7th   5th   6th   8th /
    8th / 8ve   8ve / 1st

(b) eight

8 (10)

Lento means:

slow	✔
smoothly	
held back	
at a medium speed	

ff means:

very quiet	
very loud	✔
moderately loud	
gradually getting louder	

⟍ means:

gradually getting quieter	✔
accent the note	
gradually getting slower	
gradually getting quicker	

♩̇ means:

staccato: smoothly	
legato: smoothly	
legato: detached	
staccato: detached	✔

Andante means:

slow	
in a singing style	
quick	
at a medium speed	✔

means:

slur: detached	
tie: detached	
slur: perform smoothly	✔
tie: hold for the value of both notes	

9 (a) (10)

(i) G

(ii) Bar 6 / 7

(iii) three

(iv) Bar 8 /final bar

(v) true

(b) (10)

Allegro moderato

Theory Paper Grade 1 2018 C
Model Answers

1 (10)

2 (10)

(a) D   G   B   A   C   E   D   F#   G

(b) two

3 (10)

C major   F major   D major

F major   D major   G major

4 (10)

5 (10)

6 (10)

7 (10)

8 (10)

means:

slur: perform smoothly ☐
tie: detached ☐
slur: detached ☐
tie: hold for the value ☑
of both notes

legato means:

slow ☐
very quiet ☐
detached ☐
smoothly ☑

Allegretto means:

slow ☐
fairly quick ☑
gradually getting slower ☐
gradually getting quicker ☐

cresc. means:

gradually getting louder ☑
gradually getting slower ☐
loud ☐
gradually getting quieter ☐

p means:

loud ☐
quiet ☑
moderately quiet ☐
very loud ☐

Fine means:

in time ☐
a little ☐
the end ☑
repeat from the beginning ☐

9 (a) (10)

(i) 3rd

(ii) true
false

(iii) semibreve / whole note

(iv) four

(b) (10)

Andante

mp cantabile   *p*

Theory Paper   Grade 1   2018   S
Model Answers

6   (10)

(a) 2nd   5th   6th   4th   8th /   7th   3rd   2nd   1st /
                                                         8ve / 1st   8th / 8ve

(b) six

7   7th   2nd   4th   (10)

        8th / 8ve   5th   3rd

8   (10)

mp means:

quiet	☐
loud	☐
moderately quiet	✔
moderately loud	☐

poco means:

a little	✔
the end	☐
detached	☐
in time	☐

───────◁ means:

accent the note	☐
gradually getting slower	☐
gradually getting quieter	☐
gradually getting louder	✔

Adagio means:

quick	☐
gradually getting slower	☐
slow	✔
held back	☐

:‖ means:

double bar-line	☐
repeat mark	✔
the end	☐
bar-line	☐

♪̇ means:

staccato: detached	☐
legato: detached	☐
accent the note	✔
legato: smoothly	☐

9 (a)   (10)

(i)   D

(ii) minim / half note

(iii) false
      true

(iv)   *legato* (smoothly)

(b)   (10)

Music Theory Practice Papers 2018 Model Answers

Model answers for four practice papers, adapted from ABRSM's 2018 Music Theory exams for Grade 1

Key features:

- a list of correct answers where appropriate
- a selection of likely options where the answer can be expressed in a variety of ways
- a single exemplar where a composition-style answer is required

Support material for ABRSM Music Theory exams

Supporting the teaching and learning of music in partnership with the Royal Schools of Music

Royal Academy of Music | Royal College of Music
Royal Northern College of Music | Royal Conservatoire of Scotland

www.abrsm.org f facebook.com/abrsm
 @abrsm   ABRSM YouTube

ISBN 978-1-78601-203-6

9 781786 012036